APPY

THE APPALOOSA COWPONY

APPY

THE APPALOOSA COWPONY

JESSIE A. CRAKER

ARPress
ILLUMINATING IDEAS.
EMPOWERING VOICES

ARPress
45 Dan Road Suite 5
Canton MA 02021

Hotline: 1(888) 821-0229
Fax: 1(508) 545-7580

Ordering Information:
Quantity sales.Special discounts are available on quantity purchases by corporations, associations, and others.For details, contact the publisher at the address above.

Printed in the United States of America.

ISBN-13:   Paperback   979-8-89356-933-9
                eBook   979-8-89356-934-6

Library of Congress Control Number: 2024907065

Table of Contents

In memory of my mother,
who encouraged me to write.

INTRODUCTION

My name is Appy. I am different than all the other horses here. My mother told me my father, whom I have not seen, is like me.

I was born in the last storm of winter. My first sight was that everything was all white and very, very cold. The wind made me think I would freeze.

As I laid there on the prairie, I shivered. Mother kept me dry by licking me with her tongue. It made me feel a lot warmer.

I am all black except my face and a long white blaze from my forehead to my nose. I have four white legs, and my feet are black. I have a large white covering on my back with large, round, black spots on it. All the colts and fillies are brown and maybe some white, but none have markings like mine.

I have been made fun of by my playmates. Some say I fell in the mud. Mother told me I am very handsome. She is all black with white feet, mane, and tail. She explained to me I am an Appaloosa.

This is my story.

PROLOGUE

The dark, threatening clouds covered the sky. The wind blew hard, and the snow fell with thick flakes. Already there was almost a foot on the ground. Our little band of horses formed a tight group with their heads to the terrible winds.

One old mare, my mother, lifted her head and wandered away from the herd. It was her time to have her foal. She shivered in the cold. How much longer could this last? It was almost time to go back to the corral, where she would be fed good hay and grain.

Alone in the white wilderness, she had me, her baby. She carefully licked me dry. Her body protected me from some of the wind as I tried to get up on wobbly legs. It was only a matter of time till I succeeded. Wobbling toward my mother, I looked for my first meal. She carefully let me nurse and then, as I wanted to lay down again, she urged me in front of her, back toward the herd where she would be warmer and so would I. She knew the herd would put her and me in the middle, giving us the warmth she so desperately needed if we were to survive.

It was late at night when the storm finally drew its last breath. The snow quit, and all was quiet. The horses lay down and slept.

Old Bess, my mother, now the newest mother, was in the middle, me tucked up to her side. We slept till morning, and the herd started to rise and feed.

Mother says I was a beauty. I had a perfect, black body, white feet, a blaze down my face, and a white blanket on my rump with large black spots on it. I was going to be a pretty large horse when grown. Mother was all black with white feet and a blaze on her face. Her tail and mane were also pure white.

I was different from all the other colts and mares there. There were browns, blacks, pintos, white, creams, and sorrels. I was the only one who bore that white blanket with spots. Mother told me that I am like my father. I look exactly like him, she said.

The other foals made fun of me. Said I was mismatched. But my mother told me I am beautiful and explained I am a special breed of horse-an Appaloosa. Some, she said, are brown with little white specks on them; others, different colors with the white. I am proud to be different, and I told my little group that I am different because my father is the same. My father was a favorite with "them."

We all wondered who "they" were. We had never seen them, but the mares told us foals that they were to be coming for them soon as travel allowed. The horses they would ride had spent the winter in the shelter of the barn or in the barn itself. Of course, none of us foals knew these words or what they meant.

I was about five days old when the sun finally came out, warming our tired, cold bodies. Mother kept me as warm as possible by licking the wet from my coat. Her tongue is long and rough, and it felt good.

As the days went by, the snow disappeared, and it grew warmer. Us foals all played, romping and strengthening our legs . We filled out from skinny little ones to fat sleek ones as our mothers fattened up on the new spring grass. No longer did I wobble when I walked. My legs didn't get all tangled up until I would fall on my nose. I learned to make them go faster and was ahead of the other foals even though I was the youngest.

The grass turned green and grew fast. The sweet smell of the flowers filled the air. When us foals tired, we ran to our mothers, ate our fill, and laid down to sleep. Our mothers kept close watch on us, as there were other animals out there on the range that were dangerous and would harm us if they could.

Our mothers explained that there were coyotes, wolves, and bears who all liked horse meat. Especially the young ones that they could catch more easily. We kept close to our mothers then.

One day, the oldest gelding, named Joe, came and said we all had to leave the beautiful pastures and head up the mountain, where there would be more food and water for us to drink.

All us foals had tender feet from running on the soft earth and grass. Our mothers gladly followed him, and we were forced to keep up, complaining about our poor feet and being tired, but he was relentless.

The herd consisted of mares and geldings and foals. We did not know there was any other type around. There were 25 adults in all. Only four of them were geldings. They watched over the mares and us youngsters. There were 20 of us younger foals. One mare who was old did not have a foal. Of the 20, there were eight colts and 12 fillies.

Joe took us up the valley and far into the canyons, where the rocks and shale was hard on our small hoofs. Oh, my, my feet hurt! Stones became embedded in the soft frogs of our hoofs, and it was hard to get them out. We stamped and shook them. Sometimes they came out, and other times they stayed, making our feet really sore. Some of the foals limped quite badly. Little Stony was one who had a bad limp and could hardly get around. That is how he got his name.

LESSONS

Joe led us up and up the mountain passes. Finally, we saw a beautiful meadow surrounded with trees, and a beautiful, cold brook ran through it. We could not wait to get our tender hoofs into the water to ease the hurt that the stones had caused. He assured us that we would toughen up as we got older.

We stayed there for a while, while the older mares and geldings ate their fill of the new grass. Joe kept watch with the other geldings. Geldings were the males who could not be fathers and had served "them." They were the old cow ponies, they said.

Joe taught us to sniff the wind to see if there was danger. What danger there was, we didn't know, but he taught us to smell any odd thing that didn't match the herd to beware. Many new things he taught us under the careful watch of the mothers.

For a few days, we had visitors as well. They sort of looked a lot like us, but they were different too. Their ears were longer, and they had shaggy gray coats. My mother said they were donkeys.

One day, we missed one of the little fillies. We searched and searched and could not find her or her mother. About a week went by and we saw her mother coming slowly back to the herd. Her head hung low, and when she got closer, we saw that she had terrible cuts and gouges in her once glossy hide. The little filly was not with her.

She stayed by herself and had her head hung down. You could tell she was in a great deal of pain. She told my mother that she had not taken precautions to protect her daughter. She let her wander at will and away from the herd. When she went to find her she called and called, but the filly didn't answer. Finally, she found her around the bend in the canyon, but it was too late. A mountain lion had killed her swiftly. When she tried to get to her filly, the lion attacked her and tried to kill her as well. She was fortunate to get away, but her baby was not lucky. She said her daughter had gone to the long sleep. She would never return.

The days grew longer and warmer. The sun blazed down on our backs, and it felt so good.

Joe said that soon they would be coming for us. It would be the time to bring them down to the ranch and separate some of the older colts and fillies and then turn the others loose again to roam until the next summer.

We would all be taken into the ranch, and that was where Temple, my father, was, and the other fathers as well. Mother said that Temple was my father and the most beautiful stallion around anywhere. Everyone said so. It seemed strange to me that he was not the father of any other foal.

Soon, I would see if I was really like him. As I could not really see all of me, he would at least let me know what I looked like. I would know, too, how the others saw me as being different.

Day after day, we watched the pass to see if anyone was coming. Who were they? What did they look like? What would they do?

One evening, as we were laying down to sleep with Joe standing guard, I heard our mothers talking together.

"Temple is too proud," they said. "Too good for us."

"He is too big," another said.

"No, he is spoiled by men," still another said.

My mother said, "He is kind and very loving."

They all laughed at her.

"No, Justin was a better stallion and a better father," one said. "No, my Rocket is," said another.

"Banjo was," said still another, and several of the mares also agreed that this one or that one was the best. Not my father. Still, I longed to see him and talk to him.

While I fell asleep, I wondered who these other fathers really were. What did they look like and would we get to see them all?

MAN

As the first gray of morning came and the mists were rising, we saw some strange beings. Horses to be sure, but there was something odd about them. They had humps on their back. They rattled and clanged as they walked toward us.

We foals all jumped and ran, but our mothers called us back quietly.

"It is them," our mothers explained. "They ride on our backs. They first put a blanket on us and then put a large leather thing that is called a saddle on our backs and tie it under our bellies. Then they take and put some straps on our heads and a cold metal bit in our mouths, so they can turn us how they want and stop us when they want. We can get them to where they want to go faster than they can on only two legs and two feet."

We wondered where the other two legs and feet went to. We were told they were born with only two legs and two feet. They are not lucky to have four. They are not too fast. They are not pretty. They have to put on hides over their other clothes to keep warm where we have our nice, warm hair. They put on what are called hats to protect their heads from the sun.

On THEY came. We watched, hidden by our mothers. The one in the front was on a dappled gray gelding. He kicked the horse and made it go to the right side of us.

"ONE, TWO, THREE, FOUR. FIVE," and on it went. "Nineteen new ones. Two are missing. Wonder what happened to those two? Wonder too if they were fillies or colts?"

Then the one who counted spotted the mare that was all cut up.

"Say, look at that mare! Looks like she tangled with a cat! It must have gotten her baby. You can see she had one. She's pretty bad, boss. We need to get her down to a vet fast. Might not make it if she is all infected like."

They went over and checked out the mare. One ran his hand over her and then got off the horse. This "they" was funny looking. His legs were bowed, and he had on funny stuff on his body. All fringes and flaps. The dust flew off him like when old Joe rolled and then got up and shook himself.

Then this "they," who was called Pete, ran his hand along her side and said to the others that they needed to get her down fast. She was not in too good a shape. He wondered if they would get her back to the ranch alive.

"Well," another said, "we need to start a fire and get some food into us."

They all stepped off their horses and took the leather things off and let the horses go roll.

Soon we saw what they called a fire. It scared us, which is quite natural, as all horses are afraid of fire. It is instinctive. When it gets away into the grass and into the trees, especially if it is dry, my mother said it can burn us as well. We scurried away from where they all sat hunched up near the fire. There were six of "them."

Presently, we heard their names. Pete; Shorty-who was the tallest of "them"; and Slim was anything but thin. He was almost as wide as he was tall. I felt sorry for the horse who had to carry him around.

Then there was Ned, who was the leader. They called him "Boss." A small one was Jerry, and a medium sized one was called Zeke.

They had been on the ranch for years and respected Mr. and Mrs. Hart and their daughter, Little Miss Mary, who loved the horses. She had yet to pick out her favorite foal to raise. Maybe in this bunch, she would find that special one.

Well, they sat there and laughed and burned something in the fire then ate it. It sure did not smell nice like flowers or grass Now the one called Zeke called out to the others:

"Hey, we got us a colt from Old Temple after all! He sure is a beauty." It was me they were talking about. "Sort of makes

Temple look shabby. Look at that blaze and those long white stockings, will ya."

"I am lookin' at his big black spots. Boy, he sure will take a champeenship someday, I'd say. Them spots are perfectly round and black. Don't see anythin' on him that isn't perfect."

Zeke again said, "He has the makings of one fine animal. This is one fine big boy."

Mother nudged me and said she had told me that time and again. All the others stopped and looked at me in wonder. Was I so different? Was I what they called a "champeen"?

Well, soon they put out the fire and put the leather things back on their horses and all the other straps. The horses stood quiet. So far, they did not even bother to talk to us. Then they put all the stuff they had taken off back on the backs of their horses and mounted up on them.

Soon, out came long snakes. Mother called them lariats. They had us all in a group with the mares on the outside and us youngsters in the middle. Old Joe was at the head of us. It fell to him to lead us home, he said. He told us we would have grain, oats, and good hay, and would learn more about life in general that fell to us horses.

Down the pass and through all the rocks and hard ground, we were pushed. Our feet had healed, and we found out that the stones did not hurt the horses that were being ridden. They had something shiny and hard stuck on each hoof. Mother said they were shoes.

That evening, as the sun was slowly sinking down in the west of us and the stars and moon were shining, we stopped.

Again, they made a fire and cooked that awful smelling stuff . We settled down and ate. Our mothers made short work of the grass and laid down with us beside them. We were tired.

Zeke came out to the herd and headed straight to my mother. He stroked her nose and called her Bess. Until then, I never knew she had another name other than "Mother."

She seemed to like being rubbed by him. He said, "Bess, it has been a long year. You and me have been apart a long time. Sure missed ya. Ya sure have a pretty baby there. Miss Mary will sure take a liken to him, you can just bet on that."

Soon they rolled themselves in more wrappings and went to sleep. Joe, of course, stood guard over us.

For two days, this was our life. Two long days. We were tired, worn out, and some of us were getting grumpy. Our mothers seemed to get along fine, but we younger foals were so tired, we could have dropped to the ground and slept the entire day away. There was not much time to lay down, even in the evening on the nice grass, and sleep. In fact, there was no time at all it seemed. Not much time to nurse during the day either. We snatched a little now and again when we could. Only when they stopped and started their fires at noon and night and in the morning did it give us a chance to eat.

Oh, we were hungry and tired and sore. This is not like playing at all. When they stopped, we hardly could eat, we were so tired. We just fell down and slept till the sun peeked over the plain.

THE RANCH

On and on we went till, in the distance, we saw some funny things sticking out of the ground that were different from the mountains, trees and rocks. Mother said they were buildings. Two of the buildings that were long and shorter were for the men. The other big one was for the horses who lived on the ranch.

There were poles like trees stuck in the ground with others across them, and Mother said that was what was called a corral. We would be put there, she said. They would give us water and food. Well, it would be for the mothers and geldings that were with us.

The dust was thick from where we all walked. Our mothers ran to the thing in the middle of the corral and stuck their noses in to drink and to get the dust out of them.

Soon, what I found out was the gate was shut, and the men left. They took their horses to another place and let them drink and took off the leather things I found out were called saddles and the bridles, which were the straps on their heads. They were turned out into another corral. Then the men disappeared into the one longer building.

One man, Ned, who they said was the foreman, walked to the other long building called a house.

We stood there in that corral and seemed to be forgotten. Then, out of the long house came Zeke and Pete. They came on and soon threw hay over the fence. It smelled good but was stiff and hard. Being babies, we did not like it. Our mothers did, and soon you could hear them crunching it between their teeth.

Funny lights soon came on in the two houses. We were left alone. Then, soon after, the lights blinked off, and all was in darkness.

Sleep soon overcame all of us after our long travel and fear of where we had been headed, even with the assurance of our mothers. We slept so long, we did not even see the sun come up.

MORNING

Morning came, and after a while, we woke and were very hungry. We sure were stiff and could hardly move. Our legs felt like they were stuck in the mud.

We saw the men walking around, and we saw a big man come out of the house. He was taller than the man called Shorty. He was bigger than the one called Slim also. "Boss" is what they called him, too. Mr. Hart.

He slowly walked with Ned to the fence to look us over.

"Nice looken bunch this year, Boss," Ned said.

"Nice is as nice is, I guess. Where is that colt you were telling us about last night? Which is the mother?"

"Bess is the mother. Temple is the father. Oh, now I see her. She is quite the mother. She is 17 years old. Probably be her last foal. She sure has a pretty son though. Looks just like his Pa, wouldn't ya, say Boss?"

"I think he will be better than Temple ever was. Wait till Miss Mary sees him. Bet she will want him for her own."

"Well, she will not have this one. He will be the salvation of our ranch in a few years. Wait till everyone sees him. They will all want him."

"Well, tomorra they will be abranden um."

"I don't want the iron on this boy. He will have the ear marking, not branded. No sense to ruin this boy's beautiful coat with a running iron."

"Good idea, Boss. Don't want to ruin his beautiful skin or mark him in any way."

So we spent our time in the corral. The mothers all wanted to get out on the grass, but they were taken one by one with their babies and taken to the barn. There, they might spend a couple of weeks in stalls. These were square corrals with a water troth and a place to put the hay and oats.

Mother was checked all over by the vet, looking for worms, and she was fed some awful stuff to get rid of them. Finally, she was led out and taken to another area. I was left in the stall.

I called to her frantically:

"Mother, Mother, where are you? Come back. I am scared! Mother!"

One of the other mothers quietly told me all would be fine. She would return in a short time.

I had to accept her word. There I was in a strange place, and Mother was not with me. I was scared and lonesome. I was only four months old , after all. I was lost in this new, scary world.

True to the other mother's word, my mother was soon led back to the stall. For three days, this took place. Mother just assured me all was fine. We would soon be back on the open range.

MISS MARY

One day the female, Mary, came out to the corral. She climbed up on the gate and looked over at us. My mother said she was the daughter-like a filly-of the Boss.

Zeke called out to her, "Miss Mary, look at the Appy there. Ain't he a beaut? He will be prettier than Temple someday."

Mary had a sweet voice, and I liked it immediately. She liked us, I could tell that. She seemed soft and pretty. She held out her hand to me and coaxed me to come over near her. I started and then ran back behind my mother. Mother told me she was not going to hurt me and that I could go over to her. She nickered and pushed me with her head.

I sided over toward Mary. She smelled good. Sort of like a flower I hadn't smelled yet. I went very slowly. Very slowly until I got near her. She made no move to grab me. I moved closer and closer until finally I got within reach of her hand that she held out.

Something smelled good. I stretched out my neck as far as it would go and took another deep smell. Oh, how wonderful it was.

Still , I could not get at what she had. My Mother nickered quietly, "go get it son, she won't hurt you."

Finally, I could stand it no more. I moved right up to her and sniffed her hand. She opened it, and oh! I quickly put my mouth over what she presented to me. So sweet, so good! It was heaven.

She said sweetly, "It is sugar, Appy."

I wondered what sugar was, and what was an Appy? Then she called to the men.

"Appy took the sugar from me. You think I could go inside with him?"

Slim came over and looked at me.

"Why sure thing. I will get a halter, and you can try some trainen on um."

He left, and two of the others, Shorty and Zeke, came over. They had a rope in their hands, and before I knew it, they had put a noose over my neck. It got tight.

"Mother!" I squealed. "Help me!"

Mother said, "It's okay, son. It will not hurt you if you just stand there and obey them. You have to learn not to fight the rope, son." Then they came and stood on each side of me and rubbed me behind the ears. It felt good. The rope was still tight on my neck.

"Here tis men," said Slim. The two men next to me took this strap all folded up and put my nose and head into it. Another one went under my jaw.

Now this was just too much for me to accept. I quickly backed up, but the rope stopped me. I jumped and kicked and squealed, but still the rope held. Now this thing on my face was pulling on me too.

"Scrappy little guy, ain't he, Miss Mary?"

"He is only about five months, I'd say."

"Ya, but he has his daddy beat already for spirit!"

"Beauty too."

Finally, Miss Mary came into the corral and took the halter and the rope. She carefully removed the other rope from my neck. Then she ran her hands down my sides and neck and finally gave me another piece of that good sugar.

Well, maybe I would let her touch me, but not those cowboys. Their hands were heavier, and they did not give me any good stuff either.

Miss Mary urged me to follow her, and before long, we were walking all around the corral. Then she took me to the gate.

"Open it, Shorty, please!"

"Well now, Miss Mary, you sure you want us to open it up? He might run away."

"Well, he sure would not run far. His mama is in the corral, now isn't she?"

So now the gate was open. Freedom!

No, my mother was behind me in the fence. She led me out. Now I bulked. I wanted to get to my mother's side, fast. I was getting hungry and tired and just wanted her comforting lick.

Still, Miss Mary persisted, and I finally got another piece of that sweet stuff. I decided to follow her as long as I did not lose sight of Mother.

Days came and went. I was led around and trained to do some things, like back up when I was told. I knew Miss Mary would not hurt me, and she would put the two straps over my back and cross them, so I would know which way to turn when she just touched my neck with them. I got to look forward to seeing her, as she always treated me with sugar cubes.

BACK TO FREEDOM

The day came when we were all back at the corral. It was a windy, dark, rainy day. The cowboys, as we learned to call them, came out with flapping blankets on that shed the rain off them.

Shorty yelled, "Open the gates!"

He was on a chestnut gelding. They never bothered with the mares and us. They were busy all the time. Hard work every day. They did say they were happy when winter came, and they would be set out to pasture and be free till spring. No work. Then they would be rounded up and brought back to work for another year. Only one horse for each cowboy stayed in the barn. These horses were fed hay all winter, and of course the four horses who were larger who pulled the Boss's wagons and buggies were kept there.

Of course, Temple and the other stallions were kept in their stalls. Each had a paddock attached that they could go out as they wanted, but they could not be free to roam the prairie like we were allowed to do. These horses were special to the Boss. The paddocks were for their exercise. Sometimes the cowboys rode them to exercise them or to the town farther away.

Shorty rode in and chased all the mares and us youngsters out with a rope he called his lariat.

Oh, how our mothers were happy to get out of the corral and run. Shorty was joined by two of the other cowboys.

Zeke and Jerry came up from behind as well. We were kept running for about two miles until we settled down to a fast walk.

Home. We were going back home. Home to the wilds of the plains, canyons, and hills. Home is where Joe took us. Funny. Old Joe was missing.

We got back to our home range and fell to eating the nice, green grass. Even I enjoyed it. It was beginning to brown some, and the flowers were all different colors now than when we were there before, and they even smelled different.

I was eating grass alongside my mother. Between times, I would still nurse from Mother and would for several more months, and then she would break me of that. Grass then would be my only food.

We were relaxed and enjoyed the time in the plains. No gelding joined our group this time. Several times, we saw one of the cowboys checking on us, but none came near us.

The days were lazy days. We all played and ran around. Slept long sleeps and got up and ran some more.

Every now and again, I would get a funny feeling. I wanted to be in the corral at the ranch and have Miss Mary come and give me a treat. I really longed to be with her. I knew it would be a long time before I was back in the corral with Miss Mary leading me around and feeding me sugar. Mother said it would be after a long winter and a part of the spring. I didn't know how long that would be, so just let it go and went to play.

As the days went by, I started to forget the treats and Mary. I forgot about the barns and the men and all that went on at the home place.

We met other animals. Some were called antelopes; some huge, shaggy creatures were called buffalo. We steered clear of the buffalo, as they were mean tempered beasts who would charge you and you had to run to escape their deadly horns. One friend of mine, a bay colt, was not fast enough and got a buffalo mad, and he got gored in the shoulder. He limped for a long time after that and bore such a terrible scar.

There were the elk with enormous antlers, but they seemed to ignore us. They were big giants, and their antlers spread out like the limbs of trees. What a weight to have to carry on their heads, but they didn't seem to mind. Mother said the big males lost their antlers come wintertime.

Of course, there were the bear and coyotes and the wolves, and also the mountain lions. We saw what a mountain lion could do. So far, we did not see any bear or wolves. Coyotes were around and screamed all night long. My mother called it howling. She said they were calling the whole family together to feed on a kill they had made.

It was getting colder now. Nights were chilly, and I snuggled up next to Mother to get warm. I noticed how thick and curly she was getting. She explained to me I was also changing to a heavier winter coat. I would need it to keep warm soon. Of course, I did not see myself. I saw the other colts and fillies were also getting shaggy.

Then one morning, I woke up and the world was all white. Snow had come again. What a disappointment. The grass was covered in white cold snow. Mother said it was frost and would go away soon with the heat of the sunshine. It did finally, about mid-morning. It was cold and wet, and the grass was stiff. It crackled under our feet as we ran and played about to keep warm.

I looked up at the mountains, and they were wearing a coat of white too on the top. My mother said it was snow there. It did not dry up and go away with the sun. It was too cold up there.

Then the leaves on the trees changed to beautiful golds and reds and even browns. Intermixed with the pines that were green, it was a pleasant sight. Then they started to fall, and the trees stood with just bare branches that waved in the high winds of the plains. We were sorry to see the leaves fall, as they were beautiful, and we knew it would not be a nice time soon. Even the trees moaned like they didn't want to see their leaves fall.

Mother said one morning I was to stay close to the others.

"Do not run and play this morning. You stay close to me and don't leave my side. Do you understand me?" she asked.

"Of course, Mother, I understand. What is wrong?"

"I do not know. Something awful is going to happen. We can just feel it."

Out of the distance between the mountains came four horses. One of them was Old Joe. We were happy to see him and wanted to run and greet him, but our mothers would not let us.

"Is it because of them, Mother?" I asked.

"No, son."

Soon they joined us and said they were here for the winter and would protect us as much as they could. They were good souls and too old to be of much use on the ranch anymore. Old Joe said he had wintered 25 times out here on the plains. Maybe more. That was indeed old.

We settled down to sleep our naps, and suddenly, we heard it. A loud wind sprang up. Our mothers and the geldings were all alert and ready to run. We all gathered in the middle of them. What was it? What was that awful noise?

"Turn your faces to the wind now," Joe said. We did as we were told, and the wind hit us hard. It howled and screamed. It buffeted us and shook us. We wedged ourselves as close as we could to the mothers and geldings.

"We are in for a very bad storm," muttered old Joe. "Too early this year. Too early," he said as his breath was taken away.

Suddenly, with what seemed like rocks being thrown at us, we were hit by hail. Large globs of ice, and they hurt! The trees could no longer shelter us. We were at the mercy of the hail. It seemed to last forever; then just as suddenly, it was over. A huge blanket of white swirled around us in snowflakes as big as ever. The wind still blew consistently but at least not as hard.

Our mothers let us lay down and sleep. It had been a hard time, and we were sore and tired. Soon, our mothers' warm bodies snuggled up to us to keep us warm.

Old Joe snuggled on my other side. He groaned as he lay down. He had really been battered. Of course, he was old and the hail really hit him. His coat was not as thick as ours, and he shivered in the night air.

When I woke up the next morning, all was white. I had to shake the snow off my back and head. Deep white snow went up past our knees, and I saw great heaps in the snow. I knew it was others in the herd who had not risen yet. Others were busy shaking the white snow off their bodies as well. Still others were pawing at the ground to get a few mouthfuls of grass.

As I looked around, only one mound did not get up. Right next to me also. I gingerly stepped over to the mound and nudged it with my foot. It did not move.

"Mother," I said. "Old Joe won't move."

"No, dear. I am afraid he is sleeping his last sleep. He will not suffer any more. He was old, son. He has gone into the long sleep, from which he will never waken. He will not know when the coyotes or wolves or bears make a meal of him. No pain. Remember him as you knew him. Do not disturb him. We will go away now. The rest will follow out of respect for him."

Silently, all passed by the mound that was Joe, giving him a last goodbye. We walked around him twice and then moved on. We walked several miles, and it was hard going. The snow being so deep and slippery with the ice beneath. The snow was heavy and wet as well. It was the first storm of the winter.

WINTER

From then on, we plodded along, scraping the snow with our hoofs trying to get a tasty morsel of dried grass.

The winds whistled around us. The snow piled up higher and higher. Food was hard to find and hard to get. We were all starving. The other geldings did not lead us like Old Joe did. They suffered right along with us.

One day, along came a wagon without wheels. My mother said it was a sled. It was pulled by the big boys from the ranch. Even they had a lot of trouble finding footing in the heavy snow. The wagon was piled high with a lot of delicious, heavenly hay. It was a lifegiving thing, and we hurried toward it, anxious to eat. We stuffed our noses into that sweet smell and wonderful lifegiving hay.

The cowboys threw it off the wagon, so each of us could get some. We were so very hungry. We knew it would not last but a day or two, but at least it gave us some nourishment.

One of the cowboys said, "Old Joe is not here. Must have joined his ancestors."

"Ya. He was a good old boy."

"One of the best ropers we ever had too. He was pretty old. Shouldn't wonder if he went in that real bad first winter storm." Then the cowboys patted us and left. We were so busy eating, we did not notice they had left.

A week went by. All the hay was gone. It was back to pawing the snow. More snow came and then more. It was up past our bellies and so hard to move around. Being smaller the snow was over our backs.

Mother said, "They will not come now with more feed, so it's now up to us to feed ourselves."

One by one of the mothers and geldings took turns breaking the trail. The rest of us followed in single file behind them. I wondered how they knew where they were going. Everything was white, and nothing looked the same when there was no snow. I asked and was told they just knew.

"Instinct," my mother said.

My eyes started to hurt and burn. Mother told me it was the snow being so bright with the sun on it. The sun felt good when it did shine. It was not hot like in the summer, but it did warm us some.

Winer stayed and stayed. We tried to reach the ranch, but it was too hard. The snow was way too deep. We could not travel far, and we were very weak.

We saw cows and their calves lying down and not getting up again. Mother said they had also entered their long sleep.

Then we looked at each other. Which one would go into their long sleep next? We were all so thin. Our ribs showed from beneath our shaggy coats. Food was so hard to find. The geldings and mothers were in far worse shape than the youngsters. We still nursed some, but now grass that was tasteless and scarce was our mainstay. Mothers lost their milk for their foals, and then we had to stay with finding grass. The mothers felt bad but just did not have any more food to give us. We were soon starving also.

One by one, some of the youngsters and then some of the older ones did not get up in the morning. They had gone to the long sleep.

Mother groaned when she laid down beside me. Getting up was hard on her too. She could barely stand.

"I am scared, Mother. Are you doing well?"

"No, son. I will soon go to the long sleep, I am afraid. You are not to be scared. You will be a champion someday, although I will not live to see it. This is a very bad winter. One of the hardest I have ever seen. You will soon be by yourself. Try and be brave, son. Go on with the others, and they will watch over you as well as the last foals. You are my last one. I am proud of you, and so is Temple. He saw you once at the ranch.

"Oh, to be there now in a nice warm stall with hay and oats ... No more cold snow. No, don't you fret about me. You will survive; I am sure of it.

"You go on to the ranch and be the king there some day. That will make me proud of you. I will watch you from wherever the last sleep takes me. I will be with Old Joe. He will care for me."

Then she went to sleep. Snuggled up next to her for her warmth, I also fell asleep. In the night, I felt so cold. I snuggled closer to her, but she was cold also. There was no warmth coming from her body. I called her. She did not answer. I pushed against her. She did not move. All night, I shivered and cried, for I knew she had entered her long sleep.

In the morning, one of the geldings, Brute by name, came to me and said to follow him. I knew my mother was truly gone then on her long sleep.

We continued on toward the ranch. At night, I lay by Brute and followed him in the morning. Three days, we walked all day. Trembling and shaking and being so tired stumbling through the deep snow, we lost more than half of the youngsters I had played with. We lost six mothers and another gelding also. They were all on their long sleep.

PARADISE

Suddenly, in the distance, we saw the ranch. We hurried as fast as possible toward it. It meant hay, grain, and water. Most of all it meant warmth. It meant Miss Mary with her sweets as well.

"Well, lookee here what's comin, Slim," said Jerry.

"Surenuf Shorty, it is our mares and little ones."

"Not many of them though. Must have lost over half of what was left there," Jerry said.

"Pete, go get some hay and pump the water trough full up." "Ned, ya better go tell the Boss about this."

"Ya. He aint gonna like it any."

"Nope, he put great store on the mares and little ones to save the ranch in another year."

"Miss Mary will be happy though. There is her Appy."

We hurried into the corral. The mothers hurried to the water and drank and drank. We had to wait turns, as it was not large enough for all of us at once. Pete kept it full for us all to drink our fill.

Then all of us hurried to the bales of hay thrown around the corral. Oh, that hay tasted so good. We were nothing but skin and bone and rough hide. A sorry sight for sure.

Then out of nowhere, it seemed that Miss Mary was there with her sweet in her hand. Oh, how wonderful. I did not need a halter to follow her anywhere. I would go where she wanted, when she wanted, and do whatever she wanted. She then gently took my head in her hands and looked into my eyes and said she was so happy I was home. She put her arm over my neck and guided me into the barn to the stall my mother had been in with me. She gave me hay and more wonderful grain called oats, along with nice cool water.

SALVATION

I was kept in the barn all the rest of the winter. The others were kept out in the corral. I wondered about this and why, but I had no mother to talk to anymore, so I did not find out the reason.

"Well, orphan, guess that is what ya are. Gotta clean the stall now. Ya can run in the runway there till I get it done."

Shorty went to work with a fork and soon had all fresh smelling bedding in there for me.

It was so nice just to lay down even though it was still cold, but no wind touched me here. The straw warmed me from head to tail. It was so thick and sweet smelling. Not good to eat though.

I felt better and knew I was not all bones and hide any more. Miss Mary came and used a stiff brush on me and got all the snarls out of my coat. She said I was getting plump and pretty.

When Miss Mary did not come, it was Jerry who took over the currying of me. Then one day, they left the barn door open when I was loose. I ran to the door and out to the corral, hoping my mother was there. There were seven of the fillies and colts left and six mothers; all the rest had gone on the long sleep and were taken away one by one.

Sadly, I walked back into the barn. They had been my playmates and friends. I was alone in that part of the barn now.

As I stayed in that box stall, it seemed like I was alone forever. Then one day, Ned came in and told Shorty that I was to be moved over into the long L wing of the barn. I had not been in that area and did not know what it was.

Shorty opened the stall door and clipped the lead on my halter, put his hand on my shoulder, and led me out of the stall and up into the runway that led to the L wing. It was not too far away after all. There were lines of stalls here with names above the doors. I saw heads poke over the stall doors. It was the stallion block. Now I knew where I was. I was no longer a colt. I was considered a full-grown stallion. Well, almost anyway. After two, I would become an adult. I would be two come next spring. All the fathers were housed in this area. Their stalls were larger and had doors to paddocks outside for their exercise. But they were kept apart, as stallions sometimes will fight if there is a mare around.

I was placed in a stall next to one that had an occupant who did not bother to stick his head out like the others did.

"Who is next to me?" I whispered.

"I am your father," came the answer. "I have been expecting you."

I knew immediately I was next to Temple.

"Where is your mother?"

"She went to the long sleep this past winter," I replied.

"I will miss her. She was old but a fine mare. I will always miss her. She was a special one."

"I miss her too."

He did not reply but went on eating. I was too small yet to see over the tall side of the stall. I could hear him there, and it was a comfort to me even though I did not know him. He was my father.

SPRING

"They are here! They are here!" Slim came running up to the barn where the other men were working.

"Who is, Slim?" Ned asked.

"Some of the new colts and fillies. They were born the past few days."

"How many do you see, Slim?" Zeke asked excitedly. "We never seen um when they were born, now did we?"

"Well, I can see four so far, but don't know if they be gal or guy ones!"

"Well, that kind of leaves only two more to come. Better tell the Boss and let Miss Mary know too. See any more from Temple?"

"Nah. All brown ones and one white. White might be a pinta."
"White might be an appaloosa, too."

"Well, only knew one mare he was bred to, and she is dead this winter. That was Bess. She was too old to have another colt, but the Boss wanted another maybe like Appy there. He tried. She was just too old. Should have kept her in the barn instead of turning her loose. Only Appy survived. Fortunate for the Boss he lived. A new colt might of taken all her strength from her, causing her death."

"Maybe there won't be any more babies this year. Winter was hard on um," Shorty spoke up and said.

"Ned, think we oughta bring um up here to the corral now? Got feed left," Zeke asked.

"We will have to see what the Boss thinks first. Might leave them on new grass for a bit. They won't go too far, I'm athinkin."

"Hey, can we take a break here and go take a look at um, Ned?"

"Sure, Boss and Miss Mary will want to also. See you out there, men."

Ned was running to the big house when Mr. Hart stepped outside.

"Hey Ned, where's the fire at?" Mr. Hart asked.

"New ones have arrived. Four so far. Two more mares with no colts. Going to go take a look. Want me to saddle up for you and Miss Mary?"

"Sure do. Want to come, Mary?"

"I sure do, Dad. I would not miss this. Any more like Appy, Ned?"

"No. Got us a white one. Might be a pinta."

"We don't have any stallions that are pinto . Are you sure, Ned?" Mr. Hart asked.

"Don't know, Boss. Take a look see. Might be an albina instead."

"Now that would be something wouldn't it, Dad? A real albino. Pink eyes too, Ned?"

"Can't tell, Miss Mary, until we get to be up close to see um. Come on, hurry. Rest of the men are already gone."

I watched and listened as they scurried to mount the geldings standing by the yard. These horses were ground tied. I guess because their reins just hung on the ground, and they were taught if they moved away, their heads would stay and the rest of their bodies go.

I wanted to go see too. My friends were out there. I was stuck inside on a beautiful spring day.

"Missing something kid?"

My father actually was talking to me.

"Yes, my friends are out there, and I am stuck in here. It is so nice out. Look at the sunshine. Oh, to be able to run and play in the new grass I see! After all that terrible cold snow, it was nice to be here, but I get so lonesome. I want to get out of here. How do you stand it being inside all the time?"

"Well, you sort of get used to it. I am not a young horse anymore. You are the only one who ever looked like me. I guess I was a big disappointment to the Boss. I have my paddock that I am allowed in whenever I wish. I can come and go in at leisure. I can see through the fence and see all what is going on. However, I have learned to live inside like that. I never did run free like you. I was born in a barn, raised in a barn, kept in a barn all my life. Only time I went out is when the Boss took me out to the rodeo and shows.

"It would not surprise me if I were to be soon sold at auction this spring roundup, or just sold outright. I am not much good anymore. They don't even bother to ride me around like they used to. I am getting too bony in the back, and my gait is not smooth as it used to be."

"Well, I would object somehow. I just want out to play and have some fun. I want to gallop and run. I want to roll in the dirt and play in the water as well."

"That is good for you now. When you get older, things will change. You have another two winters before you will have to be like me. Inside where you can no longer run free."

"Then I will run away! That is what I will do! First chance I get! I will run away and hide, and they won't find me. I will not be inside like you the rest of my life."

"Running away has its problems too, son. Take my word for it. I know. I tried it once. It was not easy when I was finally caught again."

All day, I wondered at what he had said. When Slim came, I went to the gate and nickered at him and kept looking outside.

"Hey, Ned! You want me to loose Appy here?"

"Ya, go ahead. Let him in with the rest of the yearlings." Well, they were yearlings. I had a month or so to go before I got to be a two-year-old.

When I was let out, I immediately went into the dirtiest dirt I could find and laid down and rolled and rolled and rolled. I itched. My winter coat was shedding, and it made me itch terrible. It sure felt good. There I was on my back with all four of my legs waving in the air. Oh joy! I then went to the new grass and did the same roll over and over. I thrashed my hoofs in the air and squealed as loud as I could.

Ned and Slim stood there and laughed and laughed. Guess they thought it was funny. Well, I would laugh too if they did it. I can just see them now. Two ugly, long, fat legs in those funny pieces of cloth waving them all around. They would wave their arms and their legs in the air while laying on their backs, shrieking with laughter at their antics.

MEETING

Well, I ran out into the middle of the corral. All the others hurried to see where I had been. I told them that I had been in the barn all winter next to my father Temple now. I told of the hay and the water and the oats that were given to me and the clean bedding, so soft and warm. It made all the rest envious of me.

"You know that there only seven of us left," a little gray filly named Misty said.

"Ya, we are not even allowed to see our mothers and their new babies," snapped a jugheaded roan colt named Fury.

"Say, do you think we will be allowed back out in the prairie with the old geldings this year?" asked another filly called Babe.

"Without our mothers?" a smallish colt said. He was called Runt.

Stockings and Nosy were quiet. Both were fillies.

"Well, I don't know, but I do know I don't like being locked up in the barn either, even if it was nice during the cold weather. Not for me," I said. "It's lonesome and boring."

We played and rolled and jumped and ate our fill of the hay that was provided for us. Our summer coats were becoming shiny, and we had filled out nicely.

Misty and myself made a pair. She followed me everywhere. Now and again, both Stockings and Nosy were there too. Runt stayed by himself mostly. Fury would let no one else near Babe, and she was not allowed near the rest of us. He sort of took over, and not one of us liked him very much. He bit and kicked us when he could manage it. He tried to bully the fillies to be with him. They wanted no part of him and stayed with me. Even Runt when he chose to join us came with me. This made Fury angry, and he kicked and bit more.

Ned and the cowboys watched us close. Every day, they would put the halters on each of us and lead us about.

Miss Mary came often, and she was the one who took me around. She always had a lump of sugar for me. She knew I was very partial to them. I always tried to please her. She was so nice to me. She kept my coat sparkling and shiny.

When the flies got bad, she came and put some stuff that stunk on me, and it kept the miserable biting little bugs away from me.

Spring went into summer, and still we were at the ranch. The mares and new colts were taken out. Two mares did not have colts or fillies this year, and it made them sad.

We watched from our corral as they left and called goodbye to them and their babies. I felt so lonely. My mother did not call me to say goodbye, as she was gone on the long sleep this past winter. It was not nearly so bad now, but I still missed her a lot.

"Wonder what will happen to us now?" Runt said

"Don't know, Runt. Probably put you in the pot and feed you to the lions," Fury snarled as he aimed a kick at Runt. Runt quickly dodged out of his way.

"Hey, quit that! Don't you have any manners or sense of being nice?" I said.

"Want to make something out of it, pretty boy?" he growled back.

"We want no trouble. The cowboys will separate all of us if you keep it up," Misty said.

RODEO

There was a lot of excitement going on. The men ran and yelled and sang ... well, it was supposed to be singing, I guess. But what a racket! If you ask me, they sure sounded way off and not musical at all.

Wonder what's happening ... ? was the thought in all our minds. *Have all the cowboys gone crazy?* They still treated us good but were very odd in what they did.

Temple was in his paddock when they came for him and had a beautiful silver mounted saddle and a beautiful silver bridle with jangles and things on it.

He came out prancing and looking really beautiful. He was all curried, and the black and white markings shone with sparkles. Guess they put something on them to make them shine like that.

"Temple, where are you going?" shouted Fury.

"Going to the Rodeo, kid," he said.

"What is a Rodeo?" I asked.

"Well, all sorts of things are at a Rodeo. There is steer wrestling, calf roping, bronc riding, barrel racing, bull riding, racing, and a lot more. Much more for people who come. All kinds of their food and games and fun. The kids ride make-believe things also. Some have ponies, which are very small horses to carry kids around a ring.

"Boss and I lead the parade. If you think I have been dooded up grand, you should see the Boss. We are the start of the Rodeo. Have been for many years now."

"Wow, I bet it is fun," Runt said.

"Shorty, get a halter on that small guy there and the bay. They are going to the Rodeo," yelled Ned.

"Ha! Bet you were going too, Mr. Priss. You are not so pretty now. Don't know why Runt is going, but I guess he will be the clown," snapped Fury.

"Enjoy yourselves," we said.

Well, the day wore on. Night came, and no one came to bother with us. Course they were all at this Rodeo.

Well into the night, we were still alone. We huddled together, wondering what had happened. No one came to see us. No one gave us hay. Would they come back, we wondered.

Soon, we fell asleep, hungry and scared. We were awakened by a clamor of the men coming home. Mr. Hart was riding Temple. Miss Mary was riding in the wagon. The rest of the cowboys were on their geldings, just singing and shouting and laughing and talking it seemed all at the same time.

As the men put their geldings in the barn and fed them, Temple was nearby, and we asked him what they were so happy about.

"Well, we took first place in about every event there is. Boss, well, he got top price for that bay colt, Fury, with his nasty temper. He will be raised to be a Rodeo bucking horse. The little one, Runt, is going to be a young boy's horse. He is so gentle and calm."

Fury and Runt ... never coming back? It was unheard of! First the others went to the long sleep, and now these two were sold and gone for good? We didn't much miss Fury, but Runt was a nice colt.

"Oh my!" cried Misty. "Will we have to go too?"

"No, my little one. No need to worry yourself. You will soon grow into mares and take the places of those who were lost last winter. Appy here will be kept for my job when he is older."

"Well at least they did not sell you yet," I said.

"No, not this year and probably not next. I heard them say that. Then you will be groomed to take my place. Don't know if they will sell me or put me to pasture."

"I won't be here. I will be long gone," I said. I was full of confidence in myself as any young horse could be .

RUNAWAY

Well, it was getting colder now. I knew we would have another snow soon. We were kept in a fenced area away from the ranch itself.

I told the fillies that it would soon be cold and snow again. They dreaded it; said they almost froze the last time.

Well, Shorty and Slim and Zeke came to take us in. We wondered where they would put us. However, this time, we were put in a different barn that had been new. All open inside. Dirt floors too but it had hay racks on the side and plenty of water.

"Well, Slim, this ought to keep our young ones safe. Going to go bring in the mares and the new babies this year, too. The Boss does not want to lose any more to the winter. Guess he knew what he was doing when he built this here barn like this. Lots of room, too, for the extra hay and grain he bought."

"Hey Zeke, don't forget to put up the bars."

"Shorty needs some more of that there grain in the tub there too."

"Well, hurry up. Supper's awaiting fer us."

Zeke ran around, and of course, he is the one who never remembers what he is told to do. He left the gate down.

Boy, I thought, *here is my chance at freedom*. I turned and said goodbye to the fillies. I told them their mothers and new ones would soon be here, and I was leaving. I was going to be on my own. I might starve or freeze, but no way was I going to be kept in the barn again like I was last year.

Here I am, a pretty good-sized yearling who knew everything. Well, I was more than that; I was 14 hands high now. That is to say, I was almost five feet at the shoulder. Four inches to a hand, they say. I was getting pretty big.

I pushed the gate, and off I went at a canter. No one knew I was gone except the fillies. They all cried when they actually saw me push the gate. I came to the outer gate, and that too was open.

I ran through it as fast as I could. I was free at last. No more halters, no ropes, no fences, no rails, no hay, no grain-just grass and freedom. I ran on till I was so tired I just had to stop. The trees were bare of their leaves now, but the leaves on the ground were soft from the rains.

I laid down and fell instantly asleep. I never realized that I had no adults around me to protect me. Suddenly, I came away when I heard a very loud growl behind me.

THE BEAR

I jumped up to my feet and turned quickly. There stood an enormous black thing. I distinctly knew from what I heard others say that this was a big bear. I was facing a very hungry grizzly bear.

He stood up on his hind legs and towered way over me. His mouth opened, and his teeth were bared at me. He kept waving his front legs with claws on them that were very long and sharp. I knew I was in big trouble if I did not run and get out of there as fast as I could. My escape was to the left of the bear, but it would mean I would have to run very close to him. Those massive claws would rip my sides or maybe smack me in the head. They were almost as large as my head anyhow, I thought.

As he stood there snarling at me, I made a lunge to the right side and then swerved to the left as fast as I could. Then I took off running for all I was worth.

I heard the bear come down on all four legs, and then I heard him crash through the underbrush after me. There was a large tree in front of me that had blown down. I had never jumped anything-not a fence or a tree. I could almost feel the terrible breath of that bear on my heels. He was very fast. I took a deep breath and jumped. I sailed over that dead tree in an instant! The bear had to stop and climb over it.

That climb slowed him down, and I took off running even faster out in the open now. Over the plain, I went as fast as I could. Nothing would slow me down.

I did not know where I was going, but I knew I had to run and run fast. My breath was coming hard. If I slowed though, I would be a meal for that bear.

I ran a couple of miles at least. I did not hear that bear anymore. I slowed down and still did not hear him. At last, I had to stop, and I looked back. He was only a black speck on the plain. I watched and saw he was going away and not chasing me anymore.

I was so tired, and my legs shook. I gasped for air and sank down to the ground. So tired. I fell asleep there on the plain. I never felt the bite of the wind nor felt the first icy fingers of the snow that hit me. I just slept on.

Morning came, and with it, I awoke. I found I was covered in over two feet of snow. Standing up, I saw white all around me. The bear must have gone away and found something else to eat.

As I looked down, I saw the grass where I had laid and quickly made my breakfast of it. Then I started off toward the hills.

ALONE

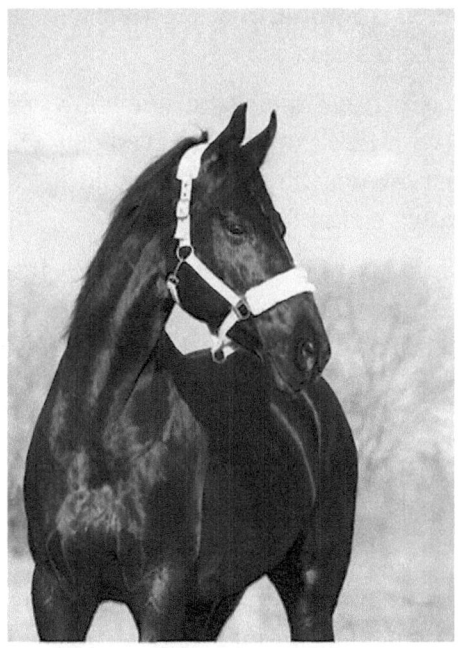

Days went by, and I traveled onward. I came to the mountains and found that there were canyons with good grass and not so much snow in them. It was here I decided would be my home for the winter.

I was sheltered from the icy blasts that blew overhead on the plains. There was a lot of deep grass, withered and brown, but still good for me to eat. There was plenty of water in the streams that ran down through it.

Day after day, night after night, I spent alone. No horses for companionship and no other animal but me. Alone! Wasn't this what I wanted?

I was lonesome. Somehow, I had outgrown being scared. I had escaped the bear and the men. I was king here, but I was alone.

I walked to the outside of the canyon and found the drifts over my back. I knew I had no choice now but to stay in the canyon where it was protected from the wind and the snow. I knew I would be alone till spring. That was a long time to be alone.

As I walked to the stream that flowed even though it was the dead of winter, I wondered if I would ever see my friends again. I wondered if I would survive here alone.

Something was driving me. I did not know what it was. If my mother had been with me, she would have been able to tell me what I did not know then. I will turn two years old in early spring. I was growing into a grown stallion.

Sometimes while I pawed the snow from the grass, I thought about the ranch and the barn where I was last winter. At times, I wished I was back there, talking to Temple. The ones I missed most were the fillies that I grew up with. Somehow, I would meet them again; of that, I was sure.

I missed when spring finally came. The sheltered canyon where I was did not thaw as fast as the plain. I did not know I could be free of it at last.

When the rains finally came, I realized that winter was over. The rain was warmer. It bared the ground, and the grass was growing green under the snow.

It was then that I walked to the opening of the canyon and looked out. Everything was starting to flower and turn green. I was free again to roam where I wanted.

PURSUIT

I knew when I ran off, I would be missed. I figured that the men would come looking in all the places I had lived. I knew I had to hide if I was to remain free.

One afternoon, as I was laying down resting, I heard horses running. I saw three riders coming toward me. I knew if I did not run and hide, they would catch me and take me back to the barn. My freedom would be lost.

Jumping up, I turned and ran toward the canyon. If I could make it there, I would be safe. At least, I thought I would be.

I ran into the canyon and then to the stream. The trees covered me. I listened, and sure enough, here came the men, fast.

"Hey Slim, you sure he went into this canyon?"

"Ya, Jerry. He sure did. I couldn't have missed him."

"Hi Pete, ya see him?"

"Here's his tracks, men. He must have lived here all winter by the looks of it. That boy knows this place," Slim said .

"Here's fresh tracks leading to the stream there. Bet he's in there hiding on us in those trees," shouted Jerry.

"There he is, men! Got our lasso's ready?" Slim asked.

I could not outrun them, and they knew it, so I just walked out to them and up to Slim. I nuzzled him, looking for something sweet.

"Well, would ya look at this? He remembers me. Knows I sometimes had some sugar in my pocket. Hand me that halter will ya, Pete?"

Well, I knew I had been caught. On went the halter and then the lead rope was attached.

"Well, this old fellow sure led us one chase all winter. The Boss was frantic. Imagine losing his prize hoss."

"Slim, we ought to get a reward for this catch," said Pete.

"Miss Mary cried when he left and ran off, that she did."

"Well, let's get this boy home. I figure about three days, and we will be there."

"On this range, who knows."

MISTY

Well, they got me home, and Mr. Hart and Miss Mary were so happy to see me, I had lumps of sugar all day.

The vet came and checked me out and gave me some of that awful worm medicine. It stuck to my tongue and felt like it would be forever in my mouth. Slim came and gave me water to wash it down with, then some nice oats to help get rid of the taste.

I had only seen the geldings and none of the others when they brought me in. They did not know I had learned to jump things when that bear chased me. I would bide my time and make another break. After getting as much sugar as I could, of course. I would miss that.

I was put in the stall next to Temple again; said they wanted me to fill out and see how fine I was.

When the vet had come that time, he said when he checked me over that I was too thin. "Winter on the range does that," he said. He said I was now seventeen hands high. That meant I was five foot, six inches at my withers. That is the part of me just back of my mane. I was a full-grown horse now; just had to fill out.

Miss Mary came in and opened the stall door and entered with her brush. She brushed me and made me feel good all over. She combed my mane and tail and trimmed the ends of my tail, so it would not drag on the ground. Of course, the only time it dragged was when I walked. When I ran it arched way up in a plume over my back and flowed out behind me.

"My, you have grown and are so beautiful now!" she said. "I will have to teach you to kneel, so I can reach your neck and back easily as well as your head."

I thought, yes, I had grown. I was now an adult ... sort of. Kind of like a teenager at the end of his teen years for a man, I suppose.

"Temple. aren't you proud of your son now? Why, he is larger than you are! Who would have ever thought it with Bess as his mother. She was only 15 hands, and you are 16. Why, you have a long-legged son!"

Mr. Hart came in and looked at me.

"He will take every prize at the Rodeo this year. Have to get him broke though. Ned, come in here," Mr. Hart called.

"Ya, Boss. What do ya need?"

"Get one of the men to put a saddle on Appy here. Put a bridle on him and keep his mouth soft."

"Dad, let me please. I will be gentle with him, and you will be really proud of us both," Miss Mary said.

"Well, if you think you can do it, okay. I will give you two weeks. Then he has to be broke regular if you have not done it. Fair enough?"

"Yes, it is fair. We will work hard, won't we, Appy?"

With those words, they all left except Slim. He came in and took me out to the corral. There was only one other in it. Misty. Coming over to greet me, she whispered, "Where did you go? What did you do? Weren't you scared? Were there others there with you? Did anything happen to you?"

My, I had a lot to tell her. I said, "Someday you will come with me, and I will show you the many things I did and saw, except one. I will take you to the canyon where I spent my winter." I never told her how lonesome I had been in that canyon though. I would never be again if she was with me.

Every day, Miss Mary would come out and curry me. Then she would take a blanket and slap it all over me. At first, I was scared of it but soon got used to her whipping it in front of me and one side and then the other side of me. Then she put it on my back. I reached around and pulled it off. She put it on; I pulled it off. That is until she smacked my nose and scolded me good. I left it on to make her happy, and she gave me more sugar.

Then she came with the saddle. She let me smell it and then feel it. She put it on my back but did not tie it on me. Then she took it off and put it on again. Off and on. Off and on. Finally, she left it on and reached under my belly and pulled the straps up and lightly tightened them.

I did not like the feel of it. I kicked out, careful not to hit her, to let her know I did not like it and would not let that stay on me at any time.

She petted me and gave me sugar and tightened it up some more, each day a little tighter till it no longer bothered me. Then she went and got the bridle. She slipped her fingers in the sides of my mouth, and of course I opened my mouth, and she slipped a cold hard piece of metal between my teeth. Yuk! How awful it was. I tried to spit it out, but she had slipped the top of the bridle over my ears, so it would not come out. Next, she adjusted the straps on each side of my face, so the bit did not hurt my mouth.

Taking the reins in her hand, she coaxed me to follow her around the corral, giving me my favorite sugar all the time. I found I could even eat it with the bit in.

Well, if this was easy to get the sugar, I would certainly do it.

After this went on for a couple of days, she put a sack of oats on the saddle. I just stood there wondering what she was doing. The weight did not bother me any. She called for Slim and Shorty to come to the corral and hold me. She wanted to put her weight in the stirrup. I would never hurt her. She stepped into the stirrup and then swung her foot over my back. I felt her slight weight completely on me.

"Let him go, Shorty," she said.

"Miss Mary, he may buck."

"No, I don't think he will. Just step back and let him go." They did it but were not very happy about it. They did not know that I would never hurt her. I was careful with her. She was not like them. She was small and gentle with me. Not that they ever hurt me, but they were a bit rougher in their handling of me than she was. We just stood there.

She said to Slim, "Take him by the bridle and lead him, so he knows what he is expected to do."

We started forward with Slim leading me by the bridle and she was on my back. She guided me then by laying the reins on my neck, which was what she taught me back when I was only a foal.

"Okay, let go, Slim."

He released me and stepped aside. We did not have a problem. She urged me forward with a touch of her little foot on my haunch. I went forward, and she guided me all around the corral.

"Open the gate now."

"Now, Miss Mary ... you don't know this hoss since he has been returned," argued Slim.

"Now, please."

Out we went. She rode me up to the house and called her father out. He was amazed. He did say though now I had to have one of the men teach me to be a cowpony.

COWPONY TRAINING

Now, I was going to go to school. Pete was going to train me to be a cowpony. I would have to learn how to chase a steer, pick out the right one that my rider wanted and know what the steer was thinking. I would have to accept the whizzing of a rope over my head as the cowboy lassoed it. Then I would have to brace myself to keep that steer from running while the cowboy threw it to the ground.

Oh, I thought it would be easy to learn. Well, it takes a lot of practice and a lot of horse sense. I did not have it, as I soon learned.

Pete was not a heavy rider. His hands were light on my bit as well. He did not have to teach me to neck rein, as Miss Mary had trained me to do that when I was a baby.

Now Pete took me for a run. He was very pleased. He found out that I was what you call a pacer. Both feet on one side would step out at the same time, which makes like a rocking chair effect for the cowboy. Very easy to ride. I was comfortable. Most horses use their right front leg and left back leg at the same time. I was different.

The first two days, he just put me in with the steers. I tried to think which one he wanted. I was always wrong. On the third day, I guess I had it all figured out. He would aim me at one particular one, and I would then chase it. I was shown how to separate it from the others while he then took the rope and roped it around its neck. Once that was done, I was to brace myself and stop fast and keep my legs braced stiff, so it could not get up and he could jump off and tie its legs together. It took some doing on my part. I would back up and keep the rope tight. I would get praises for it and sometimes a nice piece of sugar as well.

Now you know I would do about anything for sugar. Within two weeks, I had graduated into being a good cowpony. It was said I was a fast learner.

I was sent out to bring in some steers, bigger than the ones we had been practicing on. One big bruiser with long horns was a real nasty fellow. He wanted to keep trying to jab me with those horns. It took a lot to keep out of his way.

Well, Pete decided to try me at him. He got his rope out and swung it in the air over my head. Letting loose a cowboy yell, he rode at this old steer with those long horns. I thought he was sort of crazy. *Whizz!* Went the rope over those nasty horns. I put on my skids and stiffened my legs, and that old steer went belly up.

Pete got down to undo him when that steer jumped to its feet. I could not back fast enough to keep the rope tight. Pete was between that steer, who was as angry as can be, and me, who was backing up as fast as I could go to keep the rope tight.

There was only one problem. We were keeping Pete in the middle, and that steer was getting madder and madder and madder. Letting out one big bellow, he charged Pete. Pete turned to run and fell in a hole-seemed to be the only hole around too.

Well, that steer lowered its head and was about to gore Pete. I took off running to the side away from Pete to keep him from being hurt. I liked him, and he was nice to me.

That steer did another belly up, and this time Pete was up and grabbed that rope and went right up that old steer. A quick twist of his hand, he had the rope off.

As soon as I felt the rope go slack, I knew I had to get back to Pete, so he could mount again and be clear of that steer.

All that night, I had gotten pets, praise, and a lot of sugar cubes from the other cowboy s. I had saved Pete from death. I was a very smart cowpony. Most others would have continued to back up.

My, was I proud! Temple said I was truly a cowpony among cowponies. He said he would never have thought to do that.

RODEO II

Well, fall was coming fast. There was talk of the Rodeo again. This year, as a two-year-old, I was going to be in it.

Pete came and said I was entered in several of the events. One of course being the steer wrestling, and I would also be in the calf roping contest as well as other milder events, as I was still pretty young to be entered into any more rough sports. Might hurt my back or legs.

Then the day arrived. It was not a nice day. It was raining pretty hard, and it did not look like it would be sunny at all. There was mud all over.

Miss Mary had asked to ride me while Mr. Hart rode Temple. Imagine two us, almost identical Appaloosas, paired together. Almost identical spots on the white background on our rumps. Both of us with four identical white stockings, and both of us with a blaze face, white mane and tail; both of us black.

Now we started out, Pete was going to ride me to town, he said so Miss Mary would not get all wet.

We were pretty muddy when we arrived. Pete covered the saddle and let me stand in the rain. He went and got a pail of clean water and made me even wetter; said he had to get the mud all off, so I would be really stand out when the parade started. Mr. Hart was doing the same with Temple.

At midmorning, the parade was lining up. The rain had almost stopped. Miss Mary and Mr. Hart came out and mounted Temple and me. We were to lead the parade down the street to the rodeo grounds.

The road was hard. Before we had started to get ready at home, they had put metal shoes on my feet, so they would not be damaged. It didn't hurt. They had trimmed my hoofs neat and then fitted these metal things to my hoof with nails. I never felt the nails. It was awkward for a little while until I got used to them.

I was glad that they were on as we pranced down the hard road. Miss Mary held a flag that fluttered above my head. This was new to me, too, and made me a bit jittery. She soothed me and said it was okay. She then gave me a sugar cube, and I was just fine.

Now we pranced down that street side by side, my father and me. It was a wonderful time to be together out of the barn and stalls.

As we entered the arena of the rodeo, Mr. Hart pulled Temple over and stood on the side as Miss Mary ran me down the field, leading six other girl riders on their horses, all the girls carrying flags. Turning, then we ran back up the field. Three of them stayed at the other end and did not return with us. When we got back up to Mr. Hart, the other three wheeled around and stood there. Mr. Hart and Temple and Miss Mary and me, we trotted to the middle of the arena.

Everyone in the stands that were all around us stood up. Music was played, and a lady sang. She sounded better than the cowboys, that is for sure. Miss Mary whispered to me it was called the national anthem. Whatever that was. Then everyone put their hands on their chests and said some words. Miss Mary said it was the pledge to the flag she was carrying.

I stood quiet while this was going on. I never moved. I noticed that Temple was a bit nervous and moved some till Mr. Hart calmed him.

Then the three on the other end ran their horses up to us, and we turned and rode to the other three and then all of us ran around the whole arena and out the gate .

Miss Mary had praise for me and so did the cowboys from the ranch. I got extra pieces of sugar for the approval. I was then taken to a place and tied beside Temple. It was the first time both of us stallions stood side by side, father and son.

He was happy for me and said so. He said we were quite a pair. Maybe he would not be sold or put out to pasture for a while with me beside him. We were a good match.

Well, Pete came and gave us a drink of nice cold water. Then he took the slicker off the saddle and mounted me. It was our turn in the arena.

The first event was I had to pick a steer out of 12 in the arena. That had become pretty easy. It did not take me long to pick him out and haze him away from the others, so Pete could get his rope on him. *Whizz!* went the rope, and the steer was caught. I pulled back on the rope, and Pete was off and running to it. *Plop!* It was down in a second, and Pete had its feet tied. Then he loosened the rope, and I could stand quiet. He then mounted me and returned me to the place next to Temple.

There was a lot of clapping from the stands and laughing from it as well. Then Pete came back and mounted me. Patting my neck, he said we had won that event. Wow! My first time, and I was a winner. Temple praised me as well.

We went back into the arena and got our prize. It was a big golden cup. Pete was so happy. He had a real cowpony. A champion cowpony. I had more sugar.

The day wore on, and we just stood there. Late in the day, the sun peeked through the black clouds. The sun felt good on our backs. I was taken for the steer roping and then back for the final parade. We won every event. Pete was ecstatic. So were Mary and Mr. Hart and the other cowboys.

Late at night, we headed for home. Pete was singing and so were the other cowboys. If I could have shut my ears, I would have. They did not sound too good. They were happy they were first in every event and that I had taken trophies.

FREEDOM AGAIN

Well, we were allowed to rest all the next day. Miss Molly came and gave me my rub and currying and some sugar. She said she was tired so she went back to the house. I was in the corral. I had heard the men talking about making the stall next to Temple mine for good. I would have a paddock made in the spring, so I could go out when I wanted or if I was out to come back in.

However, I was not going to be penned up again. This time, I was very sure of it. Imagine I was only about six months over two, and for the next 20 or so years, I was to be in a barn and only taken out when they wanted to do something with me. No way!

I watched to see all the cowboys go inside. I was alone in the corral. I knew I could jump but never tried it on a fence before. The fence was three poles high, about to my shoulders. I remembered the tree I had jumped to get away from the bear. I started to run around the middle of the corral. I had to judge how much speed I could get to get over that fence.

I noticed that the gate was about a foot shorter than the fence itself. That was my goal. I picked up speed and lifted my front feet up and pushed really hard with my hind feet and up and up I went-right over the top of the gate! Down I came, and I took off running. I was FREE!

Across the prairie, I ran. I knew I would not be missed until tomorrow morning unless by chance someone came out and found the corral empty.

I ran until I was out of breath, then I slowed down. I was thirsty and looked for a stream to get a nice cool drink. It took me over half the night to find one. I laid down by this stream and fell asleep. The sun woke me in the morning, and I was on my way agam.

Happy day! I trotted along, heading for the mountains. I knew they would search for me where I had been last winter, so that definitely would not be for me this year.

Night found me still on the prairie but headed for those distant mountains. I found another stream and drank and ate near it. I sure was hungry, as I had not eaten any grass the day I left. I stayed here for the day and drank and laid down to sleep awhile. Then rain started during the night, and it was still dark when I left for the mountains again. By nightfall, I had reached the lower part of them. There was a lot of good grass and still green and plenty of water in the streams.

For two days, I rested there, watching always for signs of the cowboys coming after me. On the third day, I left and headed into the canyons and hills. I finally found a nice, secluded canyon with tall walls like my old one and a lot of good food and water. There was a cave at one end big enough for me to enter.

I smelled the cave to see if any other animal had been there. I did not sense any. It was dry and very cozy, kind of like a stall. If it got nasty outside, well, I would just drop into the cave and sleep till the next day and then go out again.

Outside, I looked for horses. I would like to spend some time with them. I was getting lonesome after having Misty and Temple and the others to talk to at the ranch.

I walked out of the canyon and onto a small plain. There, I sighted a band of about 30 mares with their foal grazing.

I was going on three now. Still young but big and muscled out from all my running and training. I started out across the plain to meet them.

THE HERD

vThe mares lifted their heads, and the colts and fillies all ran into the middle for protection, just like I was told to do by my mother. These mares, though, I had never seen before.

The older lead mare came forward and said in a very loud nicker, "You better scram, youngster. You are not welcome here. We have a leader. He won't let you stay here. You are not a little colt anymore, but an adult stallion. Young, yes, but grown up." Then she turned and walked back to the herd.

I wondered what she meant. I was always with geldings and mares and colts and fillies. The stallions were in the barn and never bothered with me. Temple was a stallion. I got along with him fine. Of course, he was my father.

Wondering what was wrong, I walked to the herd. Then I heard a horse scram at me. Looking up on the hillside, I saw a big bay stallion. Ugly with a roman nose and narrow eyes. He was scarred all over, and to end it up, his legs were twisted. His tail was on crooked, and he looked fat.

He thundered down the hillside with his teeth bared at me.

"Whoa!" I called to him that I had an ideal place to winter and wanted to share it with them all. He only bared his teeth and attempted to bite me. I easily outstepped him. Then he turned and aimed both his hind feet at my head. No way was this acceptable. I whirled around and kicked him in the ribs. I was only defending myself. The kick knocked him to the ground. He got up and, with teeth bared, made at me again. This time, I rose to meet his charge. The two of us hit chest on with a mighty thump.

He was thrown off balance and almost fell again. Once again, he charged, and I rose and battered him with my front feet. One foot struck him in the head. Again, he fell, stunned. Slowly this time, he got up and circled me. When he charged again, I was ready for him. I ran against him, and he fell again.

No, I do not care for bullies when I only wanted to be nice and invite them to a safe place for the winter, and this was just too much to take. He got up slowly and shook his head. I ran at him again, but this time he turned and ran from me.

All the mares had been watching to see the outcome. The big lead mare started to follow him but something in me made me speed up and run in front of her to stop her.

"Stay with the rest," I said.

"For a youngster, you are pretty sure of yourself," she said. "Just because you have pushed him off, he will be back. We all belong to him," she snapped.

"For a big-headed nag, you don't have any sense do you?" I said.

"Aren't you owned by men?"

"No, never have been and never will be either."

She started to walk away from the herd toward the way the other stallion left.

"Go, go to him then and don't return. I have a place I am going to take all the rest for the winter. It has plenty of food and good water and a lot of shelter."

There were actually 16 mares and 15 young ones in the herd. There were four fillies who were older than the others and were not with their mothers. No other older colt was there.

As they passed into my canyon, one mare, a pretty pinto, came and told me her name was Spot. She was black and white, though mostly white. She said that no colt over two was allowed to stay with the herd. The leader drove them out to be on their own. There was always one trying to take over the herd and had to be fought off.

I asked why and she said that I would soon find out. She had a little filly by her side, who looked like the stallion I had chased off. She sure was no beauty. Ugly is what I would call her. Nothing like her mother. I wondered if she would go into the long sleep in the winter.

DONKEYS

Winter came upon us soon after. Not as furious as the winter before when I wintered in the other canyon. They seemed far in the past now. I felt it my duty to watch over all the herd.

We wintered well and safe. It was almost spring when I noticed we had company. Four animals came into the canyon. Now they were small and did sort of look like horses.

I ran to meet them and see who they were and what they wanted.

"Hello," one of the strange creatures said. "Can we stay with you? We are just four little donkeys, and we are afraid to be alone any longer. You are strong and can protect us."

"Sure, but stay away from the mares and colts. You are welcome to our canyon," I said.

So these strange little guys came in and stayed in our canyon as the short winter days blossomed into longer warmer days of spring. They told me they were owned by a man who was called Mex; said he went into the long sleep after someone hit him. They had run off and were frightened. They had never been alone before. They offered no threat and no argument. They stayed by themselves deep within the canyon, where we would be their protectors.

One day, one of these came running to me and said there was something down in the canyon that was after them.

Of course, I went to investigate. I smelled the air, and it was rank with an odor I could not recognize. I said to the three to come up to the herd and stay with it for a while. They quickly agreed. I stayed behind to see if anything followed them. Sure enough, I spotted what that was.

It made me nervous. Then another appeared. Two of these animals were after the donkeys. They were shaggy and gray. The larger one had a splotch of white on its face.

As they came toward me, I turned and ran back to the herd to make sure they were all safe. Then I turned to face the two intruders to my territory who threatened my mares and foals as well as the odd ones.

"It's a wolf!" came a cry from the herd. All the youngsters were in the middle. I faced the two who came on toward us. The little donkeys cried to save them. They were so scared, and so were the mares. They were frightened and nickered and neighed something fierce.

Only one of the older ones came and stood beside me.

"Well, now what kid?" she asked.

"Well, I will protect the herd," I said.

"Against two of them creatures?" she asked.

"Sure, why not. They don't scare me," I bravely stated. Just then the two separated and ran around the herd. I took off after the big one. It did not take me long to reach him, and I reached down and grabbed him by his neck and threw him far up in the air. I met him with my hoofs, and he landed with a yelp.

Then the other came running, and I lunged at it. It did not take me long to send her flying through the air with a kick to her hind quarters as well. Then I took after them and chased them out onto the plain. They ran with their tails between their hind legs squealing all the way. They would not bother us anymore.

HOME RANGE

Then I decided to leave the canyon and head for the home range where I was born. In fact, I might just take the whole herd with me right into the ranch.

This took a while as the mares gave birth to 16 little ones. Fourteen were fillies, and two colts. They were not so ugly. In fact, they were very pretty.

One of the older mares told me that the ugly one had been boss of the herd for not quite a year. He beat the other stallion, who was father to all the new little ones. He just brought the pinto mare and her baby. They alone were his. This ugly stallion was very bad. Nasty to the mares and babies. Most of the colts, he drove them off as soon as they were born to die alone but kept the Mothers. He even killed some of the colts.

I was pretty proud now. I had a herd of 51. I was happy to be their leader. They obeyed me and did what I told them. They were safe and well taken care of.

We got to home range in the middle of summer. The colts and fillies were growing stronger. We were not far from the ranch. I wondered if Miss Mary was there with her sugar and wanted to find out. I wondered about Temple and the others. I wondered about the mares I grew up with.

Each day, I would turn toward the home ranch. Each day, I battled not to go there but wanting to. Then finally towards fall, I knew the Rodeo would be coming, and I knew I was needed there for that. I would escape again if I could.

I was drawn to the ranch like a magnet. I called the mares and colts and started out. They were scared, but I said they were in safe keeping. I said the men there would be nice and feed them and take care of them. I had something I just had to do.

As the afternoon broke and the sun came out after two days of steady rain, we saw the ranch. Onward we went, straight into the yard of the Ranch.

Shorty, Slim, Ned, Jerry, Zeke, and Pete were running into the yard. Mr. Hart and Miss Mary were coming out on the porch to see us.

I thundered into the yard and up to the gate, and Shorty hurried and opened the gate for me. I took all the horses into the corral. Slim hurried and put water in the trough for us to drink.

"Well now, would ya look at this. I sure am amazed!" Shorty yelled.

"Ya, a wild herd," Jerry yelled back.

"Mr. Hart, ya see Appy there? Look at what he brought Miss Mary!" yelled Ned who was jumping up and down.

Jerry said to Zeke, "Sure I can see it too. Can't believe it though. Thought he was a goner and would never come home."

Mr. Hart came and looked at us. I was standing alone. He said, "Well, I said when he was born that he would be our salvation. The colts here who are yearlings will be sold, and they will keep us another year. The ones who are new will be sold off next year, and we will have no more debt. Have to get them separated from the others though and have the vet in to see each one of those he brought."

"Miss Mary, what do you think of your Appy now?" Ned asked.

"Well, he sure deserves all the reward we can give him." With that, she held out her hand, and I ran to her to get my special treat. Sugar! Oh, was it ever good! I sure missed it.

"Well, Ned, I think we will have our rodeo and sell those colts, and after that, we will let Appy here out on the plains to take his mares out for the winter again. Not supposed to let a stallion loose, but he has sure earned his freedom. Would not be surprised next year's crop of foals will have the looks of Appy in more ways than one. Maybe even get a Bess from one of them," Mr. Hart stated.

"Oh, Dad, wouldn't that be wonderful? A whole 15 foals all marked like Appy and Temple."

I did not like to hear about my father. Those mares were mine, and I would keep them and protect them. They could take the babies that came. I would not mind, as there would be more. It was my freedom I wanted. Freedom to run and to fly and to race wherever I wanted to go.

There would always be Miss Mary and the ranch to come to in the fall. I would be free to roam until I wanted to bring the mares and foals into the ranch.

RODEO III

Well, it was rodeo time agam. Temple and I agam led the parade, took all the honors, and I won all the trophies I participated for. The ranch thrived. All the yearling colts were sold and a couple of the fillies who did not appear too pretty. They brought enough money to the ranch to last several years.

Back to the ranch, I surveyed all my mares and fillies. None were of my descent, so I could take them back out. Next year would be a different story. All the babies would be mine unless I was defeated in battle over them.

I stood with my head high, looking toward the plains. Miss Mary came with my sugar and curried me. She patted me, hugged me, and gave me more. Then she went to the gate and opened it, so we could leave for the winter ranges.

"Take care, Appy. See you next year. We sure do love you." Again, she offered that special treat to send me off. Running around my herd of mares and foals, I chased them through the gate to freedom, out onto the vast plains and to my secluded valley for the winter months.

Free to do as I wanted to do.

It would take us a week to get to the valley. I was not running this time but at a slow trot, so the little ones could keep up. I was the master now.

WINTER

vMy mares and I were content in our valley. It stormed, and I led them to safety of the cave. Then when it was over, I led them out again.

It was early spring when the mares started to foal. I looked them over as the spring grasses and flowers bloomed. I had several fine colts who looked exactly like me. There were four fillies also who had my markings. Others looked like my mother, Bess. All in all, I had 20 new foals. Eight fillies and 12 colts. I wondered which one Miss Mary would keep at the ranch and raise and give sugar to.

Again, I returned to the ranch in the fall. Mr. Hart was so very pleased.

"Imagine, 12 Appaloosas in that herd now. Next year, we will have an auction to place them in good places. All these will be sold except that one little filly. She looks like Bess. Maybe, just maybe, she will make as good a cowpony as she was.

And so it went. For many years, more than I can count, I have been free all winter and spring. Temple went to his long sleep at the ranch about five years after I first brought in my herd to the ranch. I had many foals who looked a lot like me. Some were fillies, and others, colts; but the one they liked the best was a lot like me in temperament and speed. This foal they kept. He was called Dynamite. Maybe you heard of him. He was a racehorse who won many races and brought in a lot of money to the ranch, so they never had to worry again.

Miss Mary, well, she got married and stayed with her husband and four children at the ranch. The men slowly retired and moved to other places. New hands took their places.

I gave up my mares this winter. I am too old now. I am in Temple's stall. I am content. Miss Mary still comes and cares for me like she always did. It won't be long before I go on the long sleep and be with my mother and Old Joe. My foals and their foals will keep my linage flourishing. If you go out west here, you will see plenty of my offspring.

SUNDOWN

vThe winter days fled on. I was content to be in my stall where it was warm. I gave up my freedom to spend my last days with Miss Mary and eat all the sugar she would give me.